CORRUPTION AND TRANSPARENCY

FOUNDATIONS OF DEMOCRACY

CORRUPTION AND TRANSPARENCY

Author and Series Advisor

Tom Lansford

Professor of Political Science

University of Southern Mississippi, Gulf Coast

MASON CREST

Mason Crest
450 Parkway Drive, Suite D
Broomall, PA 19008
www.masoncrest.com

MTM Publishing, Inc.
435 West 23rd Street, #8C
New York, NY 10011
www.mtmpublishing.com

President: Valerie Tomaselli
Vice President, Book Development: Hilary Poole
Designer: Annemarie Redmond
Copyeditor: Peter Jaskowiak
Editorial Assistant: Andrea St. Aubin

Series ISBN: 978-1-4222-3625-3
Hardback ISBN: 978-1-4222-3627-7
E-Book ISBN: 978-1-4222-8271-7

Library of Congress Cataloging-in-Publication Data
Names: Lansford, Tom, author.
Title: Corruption and transparency / by Tom Lansford.
Description: Broomall, PA: Mason Crest, 2017. | Series: Foundations of
   democracy | Includes index.
Identifiers: LCCN 2016004308| ISBN 9781422236277 (hardback) | ISBN
   9781422236253 (series) | ISBN 9781422282717 (ebook)
Subjects: LCSH: Political corruption—Juvenile literature. | Transparency in
   government—Juvenile literature.
Classification: LCC JF1081 .L36 2017 | DDC 364.1/323—dc23
LC record available at https://lccn.loc.gov/2016004308

Printed and bound in the United States of America.

First printing
9 8 7 6 5 4 3 2 1

TABLE OF CONTENTS

Key Icons to Look for:

Words to Understand: These words with their easy-to-understand definitions will increase the reader's understanding of the text, while building vocabulary skills.

Sidebars: This boxed material within the main text allows readers to build knowledge, gain insights, explore possibilities, and broaden their perspectives by weaving together additional information to provide realistic and holistic perspectives.

Research Projects: Readers are pointed toward areas of further inquiry connected to each chapter. Suggestions are provided for projects that encourage deeper research and analysis.

Text-Dependent Questions: These questions send the reader back to the text for more careful attention to the evidence presented there.

Series Glossary of Key Terms: This back-of-the-book glossary contains terminology used throughout the series. Words found here increase the reader's ability to read and comprehend higher-level books and articles in this field.

Iraqi women at a political rally in 2010, in advance of the country's parliamentary elections.

SERIES INTRODUCTION

Democracy is a form of government in which the people hold all or most of the political power. In democracies, government officials are expected to take actions and implement policies that reflect the will of the majority of the citizenry. In other political systems, the rulers generally rule for their own benefit, or at least they usually put their own interests first. This results in deep differences between the rulers and the average citizen. In undemocratic states, elites enjoy far more privileges and advantages than the average citizen. Indeed, autocratic governments are often created to exploit the average citizen.

Elections allow citizens to choose representatives to make choices for them, and under some circumstances to decide major issues themselves. Yet democracy is much more than campaigns and elections. Many nations conduct elections but are not democratic. True democracy is dependent on a range of freedoms for its citizenry, and it simultaneously exists to protect and enhance those freedoms. At its best, democracy ensures that elites, average citizens, and even groups on the margins of society all have the same rights, privileges, and opportunities. The components of democracy have changed over time as individuals and groups have struggled to expand equality. In doing so, the very notion of what makes up a democracy has evolved. The volumes in this series examine the core freedoms that form the foundation of modern democracy.

Citizenship and Immigration explores what it means to be a citizen in a democracy. The principles of democracy are based on equality, liberty, and government by the consent of the people. Equality means that all citizens have the same rights and responsibilities. Democracies have struggled to integrate all groups and ensure full equality. Citizenship in a democracy is the formal recognition that a person is a member of the country's political community. Modern democracies have faced profound debates over immigration, especially how many people to admit to the country and what rights to confer on immigrants who are not citizens.

Challenges have also emerged within democracies over how to ensure disadvantaged groups enjoy full equality with the majority, or traditionally dominant, populations. While outdated legal or political barriers have been mostly removed, democracies still struggle to overcome cultural or economic impediments to equality. *Gender Equality and Identity Rights* analyzes why gender equality has proven especially challenging, requiring political, economic, and cultural reforms. Concurrently, *Religious, Cultural, and Minority Rights* surveys the efforts that democracies have undertaken to integrate disadvantaged groups into the political, economic, and social mainstream.

A free and unfettered media provides an important check on government power and ensures an informed citizenry. The importance of free expression and a free press are detailed in *Speech, Media, and Protest*, while *Employment and Workers' Rights* provides readers with an overview of the importance of economic liberty and the ways in which employment and workers' rights reinforce equality by guaranteeing opportunity.

The maintenance of both liberty and equality requires a legal system in which the police are constrained by the rule of law. This means that security officials understand and respect the rights of individuals and groups and use their power in a manner that benefits communities, not represses them. While this is the ideal, legal systems continue to struggle to achieve equality, especially among disadvantaged groups. These topics form the core of *Justice, Policing, and the Rule of Law.*

Corruption and Transparency examines the greatest danger to democracy: corruption. Corruption can undermine people's faith in government and erode equality. Transparency, or open government, provides the best means to prevent corruption by ensuring that the decisions and actions of officials are easily understood.

As discussed in *Political Participation and Voting Rights*, a government of the people requires its citizens to provide regular input on policies and decisions through consultations and voting. Despite the importance of voting, the history of democracies has been marked by the struggle to expand voting rights. Many groups, including women, only gained the right to vote in the last century, and continue to be underrepresented in political office.

Ultimately, all of the foundations of democracy are interrelated. Equality ensures liberty, while liberty helps maintain equality. Meanwhile, both are necessary for a government by consent to be effective and lasting. Within a democracy, all people must be treated equally and be able to enjoy the full range of liberties of the country, including rights such as free speech, religion, and voting.

—Tom Lansford

CHAPTER ONE

WHAT IS GOOD GOVERNANCE?

 ## WORDS TO UNDERSTAND

corruption: illegal or unethical behavior on the part of officials who abuse their position.

democracy: a government in which the people hold all or most political power and express their preferences on issues through regular voting and elections.

dictatorship: rule by a single individual, a dictator, who holds all or most political power and is not accountable to the citizens of a nation.

good governance: the political processes by which governmental institutions promote and protect political, social, and economic rights.

minority: a group that is different—ethnically, racially, culturally, or in terms of religion—within a larger society.

referendum: a direct vote by citizens on an issue.

Governments are institutions created to make and enforce decisions on a wide variety of issues. These decisions range from establishing a minimum age for marriage to whether or not to declare war on another nation. Governments also gather and distribute resources and regulate aspects of everyday life. For instance, governments collect taxes and use that money to pay for programs such as education. They also decide how long a person should attend school.

For much of human history, governments existed mainly to benefit a small group of elites who held all or most of the political power. These elites used governments to increase their wealth and become more powerful. Rulers were often corrupt and dishonest. They used force to remain in power. However, the rise of **democracy** as a political system made governments more accountable to their citizens. Through elections, people were able to express approval or disapproval of their government's decisions and performance. Therefore, elected officials had to be responsive to the needs and desires of voters. Also, as democracy spread, people demanded more accountability from their elected officials. Citizens want a government that is open and honest, and that serves the needs of the community.

PRINCIPLES OF GOOD GOVERNANCE

All citizens of a country have a right to **good governance**. This does not mean that a government will always make decisions that its citizens agree with. Instead, it means that the institution should use the best system to actually make those decisions—one in which all policy choices are considered, and in which decisions are designed to provide the most benefits for the most people.

Good governance must be based on openness; this openness is often described as transparency. People should be able to easily understand how and why a decision was made. They should be allowed access to the same information, data, and advice that was used by governments to enact choices. Citizens should also have an opportunity to participate in the process by expressing their opinions and

Supporters of Ireland's same-sex marriage law celebrate in Dublin on May 23, 2015. Ireland was the first country in the world to pass marriage equality via a referendum.

preferences on issues to government officials. Governments often have meetings to gather input from citizens.

In some countries, governments allow the citizens to vote directly on issues through **referendums**. For instance, Ireland has conducted referendums on issues such as the legalization of divorce and same-sex marriage. Openness requires freedom of expression, which is the right of citizens to express their ideas and opinions orally or in writing,

REFERENDUMS AND MINORITY RIGHTS

Referendums allow people to vote directly on a particular issue. For instance, on March 23, 2003, the government of Slovenia held a joint referendum. It asked its citizens whether or not the country should join the European Union (EU), a political, economic, and cultural organization of European countries. The government also asked citizens if Slovenia should become part of the North Atlantic Treaty Organization (NATO), a military alliance of European and North American nations, including the United States. A large majority of voters (89.6 percent) cast ballots in favor of joining the EU, while 66 percent voted in favor of NATO membership. Slovenia subsequently became a member of both organizations.

One disadvantage of referendums is that they may undermine **minority** rights. Since referendums are decided by the will of the majority, minority groups may be outvoted. In 2004, Slovenia held a referendum on restoring rights to approximately 20,000 people who lived in Slovenia when the country became independent in 1991, but who did not gain Slovenian citizenship. This small group of people were known as Izbrisani, or the "Erased," because they had their rights taken away. In the April referendum, 96 percent of Slovenian voters voted against restoring rights to the Izbrisani, leaving them without citizenship or basic rights.

without fear of punishment. Freedom of expression includes even those beliefs that others might find controversial or distasteful. When people voice their views, government must respond and consider those opinions in making choices about issues.

Good governance must adhere strictly to existing laws and rules. Government officials must not be perceived as being above the law or privileged in ways that average citizens are not. If people believe that officials are corrupt, it undermines the legitimacy of the government and people's faith in it. Citizens may also come to distrust government if it is not efficient and effective. Once a decision is made, people expect the government to move quickly and properly to implement it.

People also expect officials to make the best use of resources. It is common for governments to be required to use companies that are the least expensive to provide services. People hold government officials accountable for their decisions and expect there to be consequences if members of the government make bad choices or are wasteful with public resources. In the United States, for instance, the misuse of public money is a crime punishable by up to 10 years in prison and a fine that is equal to the amount taken or misspent, or even double that amount in some cases.

INCLUSIVENESS

Effective governments must include all citizens in the decision-making process. In many countries, ethnic, racial, or religious minority groups have not always enjoyed the same rights as other citizens. Modern democracies have enacted laws and undertaken special policies to ensure that all groups have the same rights and freedoms. Governments also seek to promote inclusiveness among its citizenry through education. In Scotland, for instance, students learn the importance of inclusion and equality in all grades from age 3 to age 18.

Democratic governments seek to guarantee that all groups participate equally in the governing process. In order to maintain the loyalty and respect of their citizenry, governments seek equity, or fairness and impartially, in decision making. This way,

Students in Williamwood High School, in Glasgow, Scotland. The principle of inclusiveness is woven into every level of the Scottish curriculum.

people do not feel left out of politics. Equity often requires compromise among groups, however. Government officials may have to work to convince people to compromise in order to gain broader acceptance of policies. Citizens are more likely to support government decisions if they feel that their views were heard and integrated in the final choice.

BAD GOVERNANCE

Not all governments operate according to the principles of good governance. Nondemocratic governments tend to be far less open or responsive to the preferences of

THE LOWEST BID

In order to make the most efficient use of their citizens' tax dollars, countries often have rules that require governments to use companies that charge the least amount for their services. Government agencies seek quotes or bids from businesses before they award a contract for work. The agency is then obligated to use the firm that offers to perform the service for the lowest price or the lowest bid. The bids are typically secret or sealed, so that other companies do not know their value. Before requirements on low bids were implemented, government officials were often able to give contracts to friends or family members in exchange for bribes, illegal payments, or other incentives. One potential negative consequence of the low-bid process, however, is that governments are forced to work with companies that may cut corners or use the cheapest products in order to reduce costs.

When hiring companies to do projects such as roadwork, governments have laws about how the bidding process works in order to try and limit corruption.

At the time of his death in 2011, Muammar Qaddafi was by some estimates worth about $200 billion. This would have made him the richest man on Earth by far.

their citizens. Often decisions are made or policies enacted that benefit only small groups of elites that support the regime. In such cases, the average citizen has little input into the decision-making process, which is instead dominated by elites.

One form of nondemocratic government is a **dictatorship**. Dictators are not accountable to their people, nor are they or their families forced to obey the same laws as their citizens. For instance, the dictator Muammar Qaddafi, who ruled Libya from 1969 to 2011, and his family were estimated to have stolen more than $50 billion from the Libyan people.

Instead of inclusiveness, nondemocratic governments often try to exploit differences between groups in order to prevent people from banding together to challenge the regime. Minority groups may be targeted for discrimination. Some governments seek to divide people by pitting one group against another. As an example, first the German Empire, and then the Belgian Empire, exploited differences between the Tutsi and Hutu tribes in their colonies of Burundi and Rwanda in Africa. The result was continuing strife between the two peoples, which resulted in a civil war in Rwanda in which more than 800,000 people were killed.

 ## SANI ABACHA

Sani Abacha became dictator of Nigeria on November 17, 1993. He ruled the country until he died of a heart attack on June 8, 1998. While in office, Abacha and his family misappropriated more than $7 billion from the government and private businesses. Most of the money was transferred to banks overseas to hide it. Following lengthy investigations, several countries were able to identify some of the stolen funds and return them to Nigeria. For example, the United States returned $480 million to Nigeria, while Switzerland restored $380 million. However, the Abacha family claims that the money was acquired through legitimate means and has fought attempts to recover the funds.

One common problem that undermines good governance is **corruption**. Corruption can affect both democratic and nondemocratic governments. Corruption can undermine public confidence in democratic governments and cause people to lose faith in elected officials. Nations with widespread corruption often have ineffective governments because corruption undermines the ability of institutions to conduct their mission and erodes public confidence.

TEXT-DEPENDENT QUESTIONS

1. How did the rise of democracy impact good governance?
2. What are the main principles of good governance?
3. Why is bad governance more likely in a dictatorship?

RESEARCH PROJECTS

1. Research freedom of expression in two countries of your choice, one a democracy, the other a nondemocratic nation. Write a report that highlights the differences in freedom of expression in the two countries.
2. Chose a democratic nation and research the ways in which that country's government attempts to include minority groups in politics. Write a report that examines whether the nation is able to effectively integrate minorities into its political system through voting and election to office.

CHAPTER TWO

CORRUPTION

 ## WORDS TO UNDERSTAND

bureaucrat: a government worker, especially in a large agency or administrative body.

civil servants: people who work for the government, not including elected officials or members of the military.

electoral fraud: the deliberate attempt to change the outcome of an election by illegally manipulating votes or interfering with the balloting process.

kleptocracy: literally "rule by thieves"; a government in which there is widespread corruption and public officials routinely seek to use their powers for personal gain.

nepotism: appointing family members to jobs or positions because of kinship, not merit.

patronage: the awarding of appointments, contracts, or other privileges for reasons other than merit.

C orruption is a problem for all governments. Beyond the obvious problems with stealing or bribery, political corruption causes people to mistrust their government, which in turn can inspire citizens to resist regime programs or defy laws. Corruption can even trigger people to rebel against a government. Illicit behavior by government officials is one of the most significant threats to good governance in democratic nations.

Corruption involves more than just a criminal act. It is an abuse of the public's trust. In democratic countries, governments rely on their citizens to participate in politics by expressing their preferences on issues. Corruption can result in decisions or policies that are not in the interests of the average citizen and instead benefit only the wealthy or elites. It can also favor one group or ethnicity over another. Corruption may also exclude some groups from public services by diverting funds to others. This can deepen divisions within a society.

An elementary school in Tijuana. The educational system in Mexico is severely impacted by government corruption.

THE COST OF CORRUPTION

Corruption exists in every country in the world, and it is impossible to accurately calculate the total cost. However, estimates are that corruption costs the world $1 trillion to $1.5 trillion per year, in both the political and private sectors. Most of that is in added expenses. Some studies have found that corruption adds 10 percent to the cost of doing business in many countries. There are also expenses involved in efforts to fight corruption. Significantly, corruption is increasing, especially in poorer nations. Meanwhile, in more wealthy countries, additional laws and anti-corruption programs have reduced fraud and illicit activity in government.

Misuse of political power may waste government resources and make it much more expensive to provide basic services such as education or health care. For instance, in Mexico, all children are entitled to free education. However, corruption is so widespread in the nation's school system that an estimated 300,000 teachers and administrators are paid, even though they never show up to teach or work. Many children show up for school without teachers in their classrooms. Corruption wastes as much as $2.8 billion per year in Mexico's educational system.

FINANCIAL CORRUPTION

Financial corruption exists in both the public and private sectors. There are four main categories of financial corruption: bribery, embezzlement, extortion, and fraud. *Bribery* is the act of providing money or gifts in exchange for favors or special consideration from public officials. People try to influence politicians or **civil servants** by providing them with cash, gifts, or other valuables. Bribery is illegal throughout the world. If caught, both the person who gives the bribe and the person who receives it are liable for punishment.

Political *embezzlement*, which is the misappropriation of public funds for private use or benefit, may occur in several ways. Forms of embezzlement can include the theft of public money for personal use or the use of public resources for personal gain. For instance, an official might use goods purchased with government money to furnish his or her home, or use a government credit card to purchase gas for a private vehicle.

Extortion is the use of threats or intimidation by public officials to obtain money or services. For instance, a police officer might demand money in return for not writing someone a summons, or a building inspector might threaten to condemn a property if the owner does not provide a bribe.

Fraud is criminal activity designed to cheat the government for financial gain. Fraud can be committee by individuals, groups, companies, or organizations. For example, a company might intentionally overcharge the government for services.

Countries in which financial corruption is widespread are commonly known as **kleptocracies**, a term that comes from the Greek word *kleptēs*, or "thief." Citizens in kleptocracies routinely have to pay bribes to public officials for routine services, and they are often exploited. Public officials such as police officers, teachers, or **bureaucrats** are often underpaid and instead rely on bribes and illicit payments.

POLITICAL CORRUPTION

Although political corruption may involve financial corruption, it also has another dimension. While financial corruption involves the illicit gain of money, goods, or services, political corruption generally revolves around efforts to keep a person, political party, or group in power. For example, a common form of political corruption is **electoral fraud**. Electoral fraud includes a variety of illicit practices, such as impersonating other voters, tampering with ballots after they have been cast, or registering people to vote who are ineligible. Sometimes the names of deceased voters remain on the voter rolls, and fraudsters may be to able vote using those persons' names. In 2015, there were 141 counties in the United States (out of more than 3,100) in which there were more people on the voter rolls than there were legal residents.

At a protest against the Russian leader Vladmir Putin in Moscow, the sign says, "Write on every banknote—Putin, kaput." The brown packages contain books detailing accusations of corruption in the Russian government. Putin's regime has been described as a "kleptocracy" by many Westerners.

The official presidential portrait of Ulysses S. Grant, who was known (among many other things) for appointing family members to government jobs.

Another form of political corruption is **patronage**. Patronage is often used to reward individuals or groups for their support of a candidate or political party. Political supporters might be appointed to government positions or be awarded government contracts in exchange for financial contributions or other forms of backing. In some cases, candidates simply reward friends or acquaintances, a practice known as cronyism. **Nepotism** occurs when politicians secure government positions for their family members. In an extreme example in the United States, President Ulysses S. Grant appointed 40 members of his family to different government posts during his time in office (1869–1877).

 ## RANDALL "DUKE" CUNNINGHAM

Randall "Duke" Cunningham was a Republican congressman from California who served in office from 1991 to 2005. During his career, Cunningham received an estimated $2.4 million in bribes for steering government contracts to three defense companies.

In 2003, Mitchell Wade, a businessman, bought Cunningham's home in California for $1.7 million, even though the house was worth a little more than half of that. Cunningham went on to live rent-free on a yacht owned by Wade. Meanwhile, Wade's company was awarded millions of dollars in defense contracts. An investigation into Cunningham's conduct revealed the connection between the congressman and Wade, and also discovered further evidence of other financial corruption.

Cunningham resigned from Congress in November 2005 after he pled guilty to a range of corruption charges, including conspiracy to commit bribery, tax evasion, and fraud. He was sentenced to eight years in prison and had to pay more than $1.8 million in fines. Wade and other figures connected to Cunningham also pled guilty were given various sentences.

A protest march against the Italian president Silvio Berlusconi in Rome, on December 5, 2009.

Requiring money or favors from a politician in exchange for not revealing damaging information is known as blackmail. For instance, the former Italian president Silvio Berlusconi, a billionaire, was accused of paying another politician more than $45 million over a 10-year period in return for not exposing Berlusconi's connections with organized crime. In other cases, blackmail is used to force a politician to vote a particular way or to gain support on an issue or policy.

ABUSE OF POWER

Official misconduct by a politician while in office is known as *abuse of power*. This term covers a wide range of illicit behavior. An official may fail to perform his or her duties

THE MOST CORRUPT COUNTRIES IN THE WORLD

The organization Transparency International publishes a list each year of the world's most corrupt countries. The organization bases it results on surveys of people within those countries and on reports by organizations such as the African Development Bank, Freedom House, and the World Bank. In 2014, the 10 most corrupt countries were:

1. Somalia
2. North Korea
3. Sudan
4. Afghanistan
5. South Sudan
6. Iraq
7. Turkmenistan
8. Uzbekistan
9. Libya
10. Eritrea

These nations share a number of characteristics. All are poor in comparison to most other countries. All are either dictatorships or countries where democracy is very weak. Most of them have also experienced recent conflict or civil war. Several could be described as kleptocracies. None would be described as having good governance.

as required. For instance, a police officer may arrest someone, and then discover that the person needs medical attention. The arresting officer has a duty to ensure that the suspect receives medical care. However, instead of taking the suspect to the hospital, the officer continues to detain and question him, and the medical condition worsens. To be guilty of official misconduct, officials must know the act they commit is illegal.

Abuse of power may also involve an official exceeding his or her authority in a way that causes harm to others. An official may allow the use of a dangerous chemical or substance in a building project, for example, or an official might authorize a project over which she or he has no authority, and therefore cause unnecessary spending.

Sometimes politicians commit criminal activities and attempt to use their office to keep from being punished. Efforts to prosecute public officials are often complicated by laws that protect government workers and officials while they are doing their duty. Known as immunity, these laws are also designed to protect elected officials from political persecution for votes they cast or decisions they make. In Brazil, for instance, elected officials are immune from prosecution while they are in office. Politicians can only be arrested if they are caught in the act of a crime (and then only very serious crimes, such as murder).

Attempts to fight corruption have been successful in many countries, as new laws have been implemented. In addition, the press has increasingly publicized cases of abuse of power. International organizations have also implemented new policies designed to encourage good governance around the world. While corruption certainly still exists, it has become less common in many democracies.

TEXT-DEPENDENT QUESTIONS

1. What are the main types of financial corruption?
2. What is the principle difference between financial corruption and political corruption?
3. What are the negative consequences of abuse of power?

RESEARCH PROJECTS

1. Research financial corruption. Choose a political figure who has been convicted of corruption and write a report on what that person did and why it was wrong.
2. Research political corruption. Write a report that explains which form of political corruption is the worst for democracy, and explain why.

CHAPTER THREE

OVERCOMING CORRUPTION

WORDS TO UNDERSTAND

audit: an independent review of an organization's finances, records, transactions, and equipment.

libel: publishing false information that is damaging to a person's reputation or career.

nongovernmental organization (NGO): a private, nonprofit group that provides services or attempts to influence governments and international organizations.

social media: various forms of electronic communications that are used by people to share information and create digital communities.

whistle-blower: a person who reports illegal or unethical conduct within government agencies or other organizations.

Democracies have increasingly gone to great lengths to reduce corruption. Governments have banned practices such as patronage and nepotism, and increased penalties for corruption. In 2009 the members of the EU agreed that they had a collective need to fight corruption and agreed on an anti-corruption mandate for the organization. Five years later, the EU published its first broad report on corruption in the countries of the organization and renewed its pledge to combat fraud and waste in government. Meanwhile, the United Nations has designated December 9 of each year as International Anti-Corruption Day to highlight how financial and political corruption undermine good governance.

Nigeria's Muhammadu Buhari at a campaign rally in January 2015. Buhari was elected president in March on an anti-corruption platform.

UNITED NATIONS CONVENTION AGAINST CORRUPTION

In 2003 negotiators at the United Nations finalized the UN Convention against Corruption (UNCAC), an international agreement to reduce financial and political corruption. The treaty requires countries to criminalize offenses such as bribery and extortion. Nations must also cooperate with each other in investigations and in efforts to recover assets stolen through financial corruption. The agreement also calls on nations to create anti-corruption bodies and establish codes of conduct for public servants. The treaty has been signed by 173 countries, and it became binding in 2005. Some important democracies, however, including Japan and New Zealand, have not ratified the agreement.

The UN headquarters in New York City.

Whereas some politicians in the past were able to maintain or resume their careers after being caught in corruption scandals, it is becoming increasingly rare in democratic countries for officials to be able to continue in office once they have been implicated or convicted of crimes. In some cases, even allegations of corruption are sufficient to end political careers. For instance, in April 2015 the South Korean prime minister Lee Wan-koo resigned following revelations that he was under investigation in a bribery scandal.

Meanwhile, an increasing number of politicians or political parties campaign for office pledging to end or reduce corruption. For example, Muhammadu Buhari was elected president of Nigeria in March 2015 mainly based on an anti-corruption

Marchers at an anti-corruption demonstration in Washington, DC, in 2013.

campaign in which the candidate promised to launch a "war" against fraud and
political crime.

ANTI-CORRUPTION MEASURES

Both democratic and nondemocratic governments have adopted tougher anti-corruption
laws. In 2010, the United Kingdom revised its bribery laws, which were more than 100
years old, through the Bribery Act. The new legislation imposed penalties of up to
10 years in prison, eliminated any limits on fines, and allowed for the confiscation of

property for those convicted in bribery cases. The law is considered one of the toughest anti-bribery measures in the world.

Countries have also taken steps to prohibit their citizens from engaging in crimes, such as bribery, in other countries. In 1977, the United States enacted the Foreign Corrupt Practices Act, which forbade U.S. citizens from bribing foreign officials. Another example is the 1998 Canadian Corruption of Foreign Public Officials Act, which also criminalizes bribing foreign politicians and officials.

A common strategy to combat financial corruption is regular **audits** of government agencies and organizations that receive government funding. Audits allow outside inspectors to examine financial transactions to determine if mistakes or financial corruption have occurred. For instance, audits in 2015 discovered that employees of the U.S. Department of Defense had been using government-issued credit cards to gain cash advances in casinos and gamble with the money.

In order to be effective, auditing agencies usually have a high degree of independence. Otherwise they could be pressured to not report irregularities. In France, for example, the Court of Audit is an independent institution that oversees financial audits of other agencies of the government. Audits may also be undertaken to account for government property. This is designed to prevent officials from selling government-owned items or using such property for private use.

Governments have also increased training for employees and officials to ensure that they do not engage in corruption. International organizations have also stepped up efforts to help new democracies train government workers. In 2012 the UN Office on Drugs and Crime (UNODC) launched a broad anti-corruption training program for civil servants in Africa.

PUBLIC PRESSURE

Public pressure is a powerful tool to combat corruption. If citizens become fed up with illicit activities, they can take a variety of actions to force politicians or

INDIAN ANTI-CORRUPTION MOVEMENT

Corruption in India prompted a nationwide series of protests and demonstrations in 2011 and 2012. The movement sought to pressure the government into enacting an anti-corruption measure that had first been introduced in 1968, but had failed following repeated efforts to pass it the nation's legislature. The law would establish an independent agency to investigate wrongdoing among officials. Complaints against public officials would be publicized. If a public official was convicted of wrongdoing, the government would recover any of its financial losses. The law would also create better protections for **whistle-blowers**.

Demonstrations in favor of passing the anti-corruption law began in April 2011, led by a prominent reformer, Anna Hazare. Protests were held throughout India. Meanwhile, the government ratified the UN Convention against Corruption in May. However, the government also endeavored to stop the protests and used police to disperse the anti-corruption demonstrators. Hazare was arrested on August 16, but released three days later. His arrest sparked even more protests. In December the anti-corruption bill was again introduced into the legislature, but again it failed, prompting new protests the next year. Anti-corruption activists also formed a new political party. A version of the legislation was finally passed in 2013.

An Indian reformer poses with a statue of Mahatma Gandhi in 2014.

China's Xi Jinping, whose anti-corruption campaign resulted in the arrest of hundreds of government officials.

governments to crack down on corruption. Citizen's groups may mount public campaigns to increase awareness of corruption or to pressure governments to enact reforms. For example, in 2015, public sentiment prompted the state government of Northern Australia to reverse itself and establish an anti-corruption agency after vigorously opposing such a step.

Public pressure can influence even nondemocratic governments. In 2012, after Xi Jinping became the leader of China, he launched a broad anti-corruption campaign. The initiative resulted in the arrest and conviction of hundreds of government officials, including Zhou Yongkang, a high ranking political leader who was sentenced to life in prison for bribery and abuse of power in 2015.

Increasingly, **nongovernmental organizations** (NGOs) have played in role in exposing corruption and rallying public opinion to combat fraud and crime. These groups help local citizens highlight wrongdoing in public office by aiding people with access to journalists or **social media**. NGOs can also help educate the public about financial or political corruption. Some NGOs were founded specifically to fight public and private corruption, including Transparency International, established in 1993. The UNODC has organized training programs to help NGOs fight official wrongdoing, and helped found the International Anti-Corruption Academy in Vienna, Austria, in 2011.

Exposing Corruption

One common anti-corruption initiative has been to encourage whistle-blowers to come forward. Many government agencies around the world offer rewards to whistle-blowers who report financial wrongdoing. However, potential whistle-blowers are often afraid to come forward for fear of losing their jobs. They may also fear that exposing corruption might reduce their chances for promotion or make other government employees not trust them. In order to protect whistle-blowers from possible retaliation, governments have enacted a variety of laws to prevent retribution and ensure that those who come forward to report crimes will keep their positions. In some cases, those who report on financial corruption are eligible for a reward.

Journalists and members of the media have played a major role in exposing corruption in countries around the world. Often, it is only through the efforts of the media that wrongdoing is brought to light. Corrupt politicians often attempt to use their power and influence to prevent official investigations. Journalists usually have

THE WHITE HOUSE

WASHINGTON

August 9, 1974

Dear Mr. Secretary:

I hereby resign the Office of President of the
United States.

Sincerely,

Richard Nixon

11.35 AM

HK

The Honorable Henry A. Kissinger
The Secretary of State
Washington, D.C. 20520

*In the Watergate scandal, what began as an investigation of a burglary ended up taking down the
leader of the free world.*

REWARDING WHISTLE-BLOWERS

One incentive to encourage whistle-blowers to come forward is the use of financial rewards. Countries around the world have implemented a range of programs that provide cash to those who report waste or fraud. In many cases, the reward is based on a percentage of the total amount that the government is able to recover. For instance, the U.S. Department of Justice will provide whistle-blowers with between 15 and 25 percent of any funds recovered from a fraud persecution. In one example, Douglas D. Keeth reported that a defense contractor United Technologies Corp., had charged the government millions of dollars for work that it never completed. United Technologies eventually paid the government $150 million in restitution. Keeth, who worked at the company at the time, received $22.5 million as a reward for blowing the whistle on the wrongdoing.

more freedom to conduct inquires. For instance, two reporters, Bob Woodward and Carl Bernstein of the *Washington Post* newspaper, helped expose a scandal in which President Richard M. Nixon and his advisors attempted to cover up a failed burglary of the campaign headquarters of the opposing Democratic Party. The revelations led to investigations that prompted Nixon's resignation on August 9, 1974. Forty-eight people were found guilty of their involvement in the break-in or subsequent cover-up.

In some nations, journalists face challenges, intimidation, and physical harm when they attempt to undercover financial or political wrongdoing. For instance, politicians may use **libel** laws to sue reporters who reveal potential corruption. In recent years, some countries have enacted new libel measures designed to intimidate reporters or limit their ability to report stories. In Iran, for example, it is a crime to criticize public officials, punishable by a fine and up to two years in prison.

Journalists may also face physical danger for reporting corruption. Jagendra Singh was an Indian reporter who wrote about Ram Murti Verma, the minister for dairy development in the state of Uttar Pradesh, India. Singh accused Verma of being involved in a series of financial crimes. On May 30, 2015, police went to his house, supposedly to arrest him, but instead poured gasoline on Singh and set him on fire. He later died. Verma and four others were subsequently arrested for murder.

TEXT-DEPENDENT QUESTIONS

1. How do audits reduce financial corruption?
2. How can nongovernmental organizations help increase public pressure to reduce corruption?
3. Why do whistle-blowers sometimes decline to come forward with allegations of corruption?

RESEARCH PROJECTS

1. Research anti corruption campaigns. Write a short report on the factors that make these campaigns successful—and on what makes them fail.
2. Research whistle-blowers. Write a brief essay that argues in favor of or against whistle-blowers receiving a financial reward for their actions.

CHAPTER FOUR

TRANSPARENCY

 ## WORDS TO UNDERSTAND

accountability: making elected officials and government workers answerable to the public for their actions, and holding them responsible for mistakes or crimes.

civic duties: responsibilities that are required of all citizens; examples may include service in the military or being on a jury.

constituents: people in a given political unit who allow elected officials to pursue their interests and represent their preferences in government.

e-government: the extensive use of electronic information technology to provide citizens greater access to government resources and information.

national security: the combined efforts of a country to protect its citizens and interests from harm.

One factor that helps reduce corruption in countries is transparency. Transparency is openness and **accountability** in government. It is based on the idea that governments should provide information to their citizens so that everyone can understand how and why decisions are made and how and why policies are

Part of the website of the United Kingdom's Cabinet Office. E-government initiatives are intended to make information available to citizens whenever and wherever they need it.

put into place. Governments that embrace transparency share facts and data with the public so that the citizenry feels knowledgeable and comfortable when an action is taken. This does not mean that citizens will always agree with the choices of a government, but they will understand how the choice came about. Transparency is a central component of good governance.

Governments that are transparent are far less likely to have widespread corruption. When actions and decisions are transparent, it is much more difficult for officials to hide corruption or mask crimes. Consequently, transparency is a major factor in government accountability.

WIKILEAKS

WikiLeaks is a nonprofit, online news organization that was founded in 2006. Its purpose is to promote transparency in governments by publishing secret or classified documents. In order to accomplish this, WikiLeaks created a website that allowed users to anonymously upload files. This gave whistle-blowers who wanted to guard their identity the ability to make public, or "leak," documents, reports, and various forms of electronic communications.

Since its founding, WikiLeaks has published thousands of documents that governments have endeavored to keep secret, and in some cases it has forced officials to change policies. For instance, the organization released a report that exposed widespread corruption by Kenyan president Daniel Moi and his family, detailing the theft of more than $1.5 billion. WikiLeaks' most famous leak began in 2010, when the organization started to publish documents from a massive file of 251,000 diplomatic messages from the United States, and almost 400,000 documents on the wars in Afghanistan and Iraq. Among the leaks was information that the United States had spied on the leaders of some of its closest allies, including France, Germany, and Japan.

Critics of WikiLeaks argue that the organization exposes secrets that could damage national security and put people in danger. It does not always redact, or censor, the names of innocent people mentioned in reports. This potentially puts spies or undercover agents in danger and exposes others to retaliation. Also, a large amount of the information has been gathered by anonymous hackers, instead of genuine whistle-blowers, and some argue that the organization encourages illegal activity. In response, WikiLeaks argues that transparency is more important than the objections raised by its critics.

Transparency is important in any government, but it is especially important in democracies. Citizens need to feel informed in order to promote participation in the political process. Democracies rely on the input of their citizens on issues. Political leaders want to know the preferences of their **constituents** so that they can represent those views. Officials often go to great lengths to ensure that people fully understand the issues and their consequences. In return, an informed citizenry is more confident in its leaders and their policies.

PRINCIPLES OF TRANSPARENCY

Transparency is based on several principles. The first principle is that information must be readily available for all citizens. Information transparency means that reports, studies, and other data must be easily accessible. This requires governments to present information in such a way that the average citizen can easily read and understand it. Yet people should also be able to see material in its original form, which may include highly detailed or technical language and data. One way to accomplish both goals is to provide summaries of government data along with access to the full reports.

To ensure accessibility, governments should distribute data in multiple ways, depending on the audience. Meetings may be held where officials provide presentations on issues, and at which citizens may question or comment on proposals. Information may also be available in the form of printed reports and studies. Increasingly, democratic governments are making efforts to publish data electronically through **e-government** initiatives. This gives citizens access 24 hours a day, 7 days a week.

The second principle of transparency is that information must be provided in a timely manner. People must have access to materials while the planning or decision-making process is ongoing. This ensures that citizens are able to provide informed feedback to officials.

The third principle is that information must be accurate. While this seems obvious, both intentional and accidental actions can prevent the spread of accurate

SOUTH AFRICA'S PROMOTION OF ACCESS TO INFORMATION ACT

In 2000, South Africa passed the Promotion of Access to Information Act. The new law made access to government information a fundamental right of all South Africans. In addition, all private groups or organizations (including businesses with more than 50 employees) must publish a manual that provides various information, including contact information for the entity, a list of records that are available to the public, and details on how to request information from the body. However, organizations are allowed to charge a small fee for some types of documents, such as photocopies or transcription of audio records. Since the act makes access to information a right, the South African Human Rights Commission is responsible for enforcement.

data. In some cases, officials might release only partial information, in an unethical attempt to influence public opinion. In other instances, data might be outdated. In some instances, unethical officials may even falsify information in order to achieve their goals.

The fourth and final principle is that transparency requires a formal legal framework. Specific laws must be in place to ensure the other three principles are followed. Laws must not only specify how transparency will be achieved, but also what the punishments are for violating those laws. Most importantly, the laws must be enforced. In many nondemocratic states, laws establishing transparency may exist, but are not applied.

ACCOUNTABILITY

One important part of transparency is accountability, which ensures that elected politicians and government workers have an obligation to explain their actions to the

CANADIAN EMBASSY   AMBASSADE DU CANADA

2b

NO. 333

~~SECRET~~

The Canadian Ambassador presents his compliments to the Secretary of State and has the honour to refer to the Secretary's Note of today's date requesting principle of the Canadian Government for the

(b)(1)

Having considered this request, the Canadian Government (b)(1) the proposal contained in the Secretary's Note on the basis of the terms and understanding set forth therein.

M. CADIEUX

WASHINGTON, D. C.

December 15, 1970.

Governments will mark documents as classified if the documents contain information that needs to be kept secret for security reasons. In this example, a diplomatic message from the Canadian embassy has been declassified—and yet significant parts of it remain censored, or "redacted."

public. People should always be able to identify the role of a public official in creating and implementing laws. They should also know how and why money is being spent.

Accountability requires that specific standards of behavior are in place. Members of the government need to understand their duties and responsibilities, as does the public. This ensures that everyone understands the criteria by which public officials are judged. It also reinforces openness by guaranteeing that members of the public know who is responsible for decisions and actions.

If there are questions or concerns about the conduct of a government official, there must be a clear system to investigate any potential wrongdoing. Investigations not only help uncover crimes or misconduct, they also help maintain public confidence in the government. Investigations serve as a way to confirm to the public that government officials or workers who engage in misconduct will be punished. At the same time,

A supporter of WikiLeaks at a parade in San Francisco, in 2011.

THE UK PUBLIC SECTOR TRANSPARENCY BOARD

In order to promote transparency in government, the United Kingdom established the Public Sector Transparency Board in 2010. The board was created to coordinate efforts to improve transparency in all government agencies. It established a single, searchable website, data.gov.uk, that allows people access to any government document, report, or other information. In addition, the board also works to ensure that information is published in a timely manner. One of its key goals is to standardize government documents and provide data in such a way that they can be reused by researchers, journalists, or the public.

investigations can confirm that officials are innocent if they have not misbehaved or made mistakes.

If investigations uncover intentional wrongdoing, there must be punishment. Any penalties must be proportionate to the crime or misdeed. The public must be aware of the punishment, and it should include compensation to any victims of corruption. These sanctions provide a way to reassure citizens that no public official is above the law.

CHALLENGES TO TRANSPARENCY

In democracies, corruption is one of the main challenges to transparency. Because it involves criminal or unethical activity, corruption leads politicians or government workers to hide information from the public or other officials. As a result, it undermines public confidence in the government and makes citizens less likely to perform their **civic duties**. Corruption also adds costs and time to public projects, thereby draining resources from other endeavors.

Corruption is not the only threat to transparency in democracies. Involving the public in decision-making processes may add time and complicate programs. In order to avoid any delays, officials sometimes seek to make decisions or undertake projects with limited public input. This may increase efficiency, but it also undermines public support and creates suspicions about programs.

National security often competes with transparency, even in democratic governments. It may be necessary to prevent some information from becoming public in order protect the nation from its enemies. For instance, the names of spies or the details of undercover operations are typically kept secret.

In nondemocratic nations, governments seldom embrace transparency, since they seek to limit the influence of their citizens on public programs and projects. Efforts to control information may extend beyond official documents and include attempts to suppress private media outlets and journalists. For instance, many nondemocratic nations tightly control the Internet and social media.

TEXT-DEPENDENT QUESTIONS

1. What are the principles of transparency?
2. What role do investigations play in accountability?
3. What are the main challenges to transparency in democratic countries?

RESEARCH PROJECTS

1. Research e-government efforts in your community, at the local, state, or national level. Write a report on how easy it is to use government websites and how those sites could be improved.
2. Research one instance in which national security led to reduced transparency. Write a brief essay that examines whether or not the government took appropriate action.

CHAPTER FIVE

INCREASING TRANSPARENCY

 ## WORDS TO UNDERSTAND

election: the process of selecting people to serve in public office through voting.

incumbent: an official who currently holds office.

judiciary: the judges and other legal components of a nation's court system.

parliament: the national legislature of some countries, such as the United Kingdom; the British Parliament served as the model for the legislatures of a number of other countries, including Australia, Canada, and New Zealand.

sunshine laws: measures designed to enhance transparency by requiring governments to conduct meetings, votes, and other business in public, or to make public records of those actions.

watchdog: a government organization charged with investigating, stopping, and, if necessary, prosecuting corruption, wrongdoing, or waste.

The Internet and the rise of electronic media have made it easier to find information on almost any given topic. Search engines such as Google or Yahoo and sites such as *Wikipedia* allow users to research laws, government programs, and individual politicians and officials. At the same time, social media provides a way for leaders, governments, public officials, and even private citizens, to distribute information, highlight corruption, or even organize the public. For instance, the leaders of many democratic countries routinely tweet about their activities or stances on various positions.

The ease with which most people can access information online has dramatically increased, vastly improving government transparency. In the past, people often had to visit government offices to obtain information about services or projects, but they can now find those documents and data online. This includes information that had been unavailable in the past.

FOIPA Request No.: 1324616-000
Subject: BLACK LIVES MATTER PROTEST
(MALL OF AMERICA BLOOMINGTON, MN
DECEMBER 20, 2014)

Dear Mr. Webster:

This acknowledges receipt of your Freedom of Information Acts (FOIA) request to the FBI.

☑ Your request has been received at FBI Headquarters for processing.

☐ Your request has been received at the [_____ Resident Agency / _____ Field Office] and forwarded to FBI Headquarters for processing.

☑ We are searching the indices to our Central Records System for the information responsive to this request. We will inform you of the results in future correspondence.

☑ Your request for a fee waiver is being considered and you will be advised of the decision at a later date.

U.S. Department of Justice
Federal Bureau of Investigation

170 Marcel Drive
Winchester, VA 22602-4843

Official Business
Penalty for Private Use $300

NOVA
VA 220
23 MAR '15
PM 4 L

When a U.S. citizen files a Freedom of Information Act request, the government is required to respond. This letter, responding to a request for information on the "Black Lives Matter" protests, indicates that the FBI will consider releasing the requested documents and reply later.

NARENDRA MODI'S TWEETS

The prime minister of India, Narendra Modi, joined Twitter in 2009 and has been an active user ever since. By 2015 he had more than 14.5 million followers. His tweets serve to promote his political agenda, but they also allow his followers to better understand his personality. The prime minister has tweeted about topics ranging from climate change to good governance to the game of cricket. Modi has also used Twitter to interact with other world leaders, including the Japanese prime minister Shinzō Abe. Such actions help increase transparency and openness and allow a high degree of interaction, including retweets.

Narendra Modi, prime minister and prolific tweeter.

Citizens, journalists, or organizations in many countries are able to access information that has not been made public by means of a "freedom of information" request. These formal requests require governments to grant access to materials or explain why they need to be kept secret or unavailable. Often, national security is cited as a reason to prevent the release of documents. Freedom of information requests have emerged as an important tool for journalists to publicize material that the public often did not know existed. For instance, freedom of information requests in the United Kingdom in 2009 allowed reporters to undercover a major scandal in which members of the British **Parliament** illegally overcharged taxpayers for expenses related to their offices. Seven members of Parliament received prison sentences for their actions.

ELECTIONS

The main way to increase transparency and accountability is through **elections**. Regular elections provide people with an opportunity to express their approval or disapproval of politicians and political parties. Elections force politicians to defend their record of accomplishments before balloting takes place. Challengers to office holders will question their decisions and policies and prompt the **incumbent** to defend his or her choices.

Elected officials generally want to remain in office, and they therefore have an incentive to respond to the preferences and desires of voters. Politicians who ignore voters may find themselves turned out of office. In some cases, special elections, known as "recalls," allow voters to remove politicians before their term is complete. Recall elections provide voters a direct way to register their displeasure with elected officials.

Politicians who are seen as corrupt are likely to be voted out of office. For instance, widespread political corruption in Bulgaria led the ruling United Democratic Forces party to lose 86 seats in the 2001 election. It retained just 51 seats. Meanwhile, a newly formed anti-corruption party, the National Movement for Stability and Progress, won 120 seats in the 240-seat parliament.

Nondemocratic countries do not hold meaningful elections. Consequently, one of the most powerful ways to ensure transparency and accountability is not available in those nations. Instead, governments and government officials have little outside pressure to engage in good governance through transparency and accountability.

INDEPENDENT OVERSIGHT

Independent oversight of government agencies can also be an effective way to increase transparency. As previously discussed, audits by outside groups are a good way to fight corruption. Audits can also increase transparency, especially if the results of that reporting are made public. A national audit of the Kenyan government in 2013–2014

The U.S. Government Accountability Office was founded in 1921; it is often called "the congressional watchdog."

found that just 1.2 percent of the budget could be properly accounted for. The Ministry of Health could not account for more than $215.5 billion in expenses.

Governments can also create independent **watchdog** organizations to oversee the financial operations of government agencies. For example, in the United States the main watchdog is the Government Accountability Office (GAO). The GAO investigates financial operations of the U.S. government and sets and enforces standards of accountability. In the United Kingdom, those functions are overseen by the National Audit Office (the same title used in Australia).

An independent **judiciary** also serves to increase transparency. The courts help enforce rules and laws on ethical behavior by government officials and agencies. Judges can force governments to act on freedom of information requests and turn over documents for public scrutiny. They also provide a forum for people to turn to when other branches of government have not acted properly. Courts also have to be transparent to be effective. One effort to improve the transparency of courts has been to televise hearings.

SUNSHINE LAWS

Sunshine laws are one of the most effective legislative tools to bolster transparency. These measures ensure that government business is done publicly, and that the public has an opportunity to understand why decisions were made and why certain policies were

SHOULD COURT PROCEEDINGS BE TELEVISED?

Proponents of televising court proceedings argue that broadcasting trials would have several benefits. It would increase transparency by making the judicial process open to the public. People could see a trial firsthand without having to rely on reports by the media. Judges, lawyers, and other participants would be more likely to behave if they knew the public was watching. They would also be better prepared. Televised trials could also help educate the public on the judicial system. On the other hand, opponents fear that witnesses might be hesitant to testify if they know they will be on camera, especially in cases where they might fear retribution. Judges, lawyers, witnesses, and other participants might play to the camera in an effort to enhance their image before the public. Finally, cameras might be an invasion of privacy for those involved.

Countries such as Brazil, Canada, and the United Kingdom routinely broadcast court hearings, in some cases even providing webcasts. In the United States, all 50 states allow cameras in some courts, but the rules vary from state to state, and there are some restrictions. The nation's highest court, the Supreme Court, does not televise its proceedings, although it provides audio and written transcripts.

PRESIDENTIAL RESIGNATIONS

As noted in an earlier chapter, elections are not the only way for the public to force political change in democracies. Public opinion, protests, and other forms of public pressure may prompt changes in government. In some cases, revelations of corruption may force politicians, including presidents, to resign. In September 2015 the president of Guatemala, Otto Pérez Molina, resigned after evidence emerged that he was involved in a widespread corruption scandal in which official took bribes in exchange for reducing taxes on goods imported into the country. The scandal also forced the resignation of the country's vice president, Roxana Baldetti, and more than 20 other officials and businessmen.

Otto Pérez Molina, former president of Guatemala.

pursued. For instance, sunshine laws might require that city council meetings be open to the public. One widely used method to help comply with sunshine law requirements is to televise meetings and legislative sessions. Many democracies have government-access television channels that broadcast live sessions of local and national governments. In addition, through e-government, officials can make documents available or even provide a library of past meetings.

In order to work, sunshine laws should ensure that there is advance notice of government meetings, so that people can make arrangements to attend. In addition, meetings should also be held in places where the public can easily be present.

Sunshine laws are not absolute, however. Some government agencies, including the military or law enforcement, do not open their operations to public scrutiny. For instance, if the police opened their meetings and documents to everyone, it would be easy for criminals to undermine investigations. There are also usually exceptions for emergency meetings or sessions that include private or privileged information.

Sunshine laws are just one of several methods that democratic governments use to enhance their transparency and openness. For democracies to have good governance, they must invest in transparency and accountability in order to suppress corruption and maintain the support of the public.

TEXT-DEPENDENT QUESTIONS

1. What is the main way for countries to increase transparency?
2. How does an independent judiciary enhance transparency?
3. In what cases are there exemptions to sunshine laws?

RESEARCH PROJECTS

1. Research cameras in courtrooms. Create a chart that presents the positive and negative aspects of having court proceedings broadcast.
2. Research your local government and find out when its next meeting occurs (or the meeting of one of its agencies). Attend that session and write a brief report of the experience, including what was on the agenda.

FURTHER READING

BOOKS

Goldstein, Brett, and Lauren Dyson, eds. *Beyond Transparency: Open Data and the Future of Civic Innovation.* San Francisco: Code for America Press, 2013.

Lathrop, Daniel, and Laurel Ruma, eds. *Open Government: Collaboration, Transparency, and Participation in Practice.* Sebastopol, CA: O'Reilly Media, 2010.

Noveck, Beth Simone. *Wiki Government: How Technology Can Make Government Better, Democracy Stronger, and Citizens More Powerful.* Washington, DC: Brookings Institution Press, 2009.

Rose-Ackerman, Susan. *Corruption and Government: Causes, Consequences, and Reform.* Cambridge, UK: Cambridge University Press, 1999.

ONLINE

Lessig, Lawrence. "Against Transparency." New Republic, October 9, 2009. http://www.newrepublic.com/article/books-and-arts/against-transparency.

Sunlight Foundation. http://sunlightfoundation.com/.

Transparency International. https://www.transparency.org/.

World Bank. "Transparency, Accountability, and Corruption in the Public Sector." http://data.worldbank.org/indicator/IQ.CPA.TRAN.XQ.

SERIES GLOSSARY

accountability: making elected officials and government workers answerable to the public for their actions, and holding them responsible for mistakes or crimes.

amnesty: a formal reprieve or pardon for people accused or convicted of committing crimes.

anarchist: a person who believes that government should be abolished because it enslaves or otherwise represses people.

assimilation: the process through which immigrants adopt the cultural, political, and social beliefs of a new nation.

autocracy: a system of government in which a small circle of elites holds most, if not all, political power.

belief: an acceptance of a statement or idea concerning a religion or faith.

citizenship: formal recognition that an individual is a member of a political community.

civil law: statutes and rules that govern private rights and responsibilities and regulate noncriminal disputes over issues such as property or contracts.

civil rights: government-protected liberties afforded to all people in democratic countries.

civil servants: people who work for the government, not including elected officials or members of the military.

corruption: illegal or unethical behavior on the part of officials who abuse their position.

democracy: A government in which the people hold all or most political power and express their preferences on issues through regular voting and elections.

deportation: the legal process whereby undocumented immigrants or those who have violated residency laws are forced to leave their new country.

dual citizenship: being a full citizen of two or more countries.

election: the process of selecting people to serve in public office through voting.

expatriate: someone who resides in a country other than his or her nation of birth.

feminism: the belief in social, economic, and political equality for women.

gender rights: providing access to equal rights for all members of a society regardless of their gender.

glass ceiling: obstacles that prevent the advancement of disadvantaged groups from obtaining senior positions of authority in business, government, and education.

globalization: a trend toward increased interconnectedness between nations and cultures across the world; globalization impacts the spheres of politics, economics, culture, and mass media.

guest workers: citizens of one country who have been granted permission to temporarily work in another nation.

homogenous: a region or nation where most people have the same ethnicity, language, religion, customs, and traditions.

human rights: rights that everyone has, regardless of birthplace or citizenship.

incumbent: an official who currently holds office.

industrialization: the transformation of social life resulting from the technological and economic developments involving factories.

jurisdiction: the official authority to administer justice through activities such as investigations, arrests, and obtaining testimony.

minority: a group that is different—ethnically, racially, culturally, or in terms of religion—within a larger society.

national security: the combined efforts of a country to protect its citizens and interests from harm.

naturalization: the legal process by which a resident noncitizen becomes a citizen of a country.

nongovernmental organization (NGO): a private, nonprofit group that provides services or attempts to influence governments and international organizations.

oligarchy: a country in which political power is held by a small, powerful, but unelected group of leaders.

partisanship: a strong bias or prejudice toward one set of beliefs that often results in an unwillingness to compromise or accept alternative points of view.

refugees: people who are kicked out of their country or forced to flee to another country because they are not welcome or fear for their lives.

right-to-work laws: laws in the United States that forbid making union membership a condition for employment.

secular state: governments that are not officially influenced by religion in making decisions.

sexism: system of beliefs, or ideology, that asserts the inferiority of one sex and justifies discrimination based on gender.

socialist: describes a political system in which major businesses or industries are owned or regulated by the community instead of by individuals or privately owned companies.

socioeconomic status: the position of a person within society, based on the combination of their income, wealth, education, family background, and social standing.

sovereignty: supreme authority over people and geographic space. National governments have sovereignty over their citizens and territory.

theocracy: a system of government in which all major decisions are made under the guidance of religious leaders' interpretation of divine authority.

treason: the betrayal of one's country.

tyranny: rule by a small group or single person.

veto: the ability to reject a law or other measure enacted by a legislature.

wage gap: the disparity in earnings between men and women for their work.

INDEX

ABOUT THE AUTHOR

Tom Lansford is a Professor of Political Science, and a former academic dean, at the University of Southern Mississippi, Gulf Coast. He is a member of the governing board of the National Social Science Association and a state liaison for Mississippi for Project Vote Smart. His research interests include foreign and security policy, and the U.S. presidency. Dr. Lansford is the author, coauthor, editor or coeditor of more than 40 books, and the author of more than one hundred essays, book chapters, encyclopedic entries, and reviews. Recent sole-authored books include: *A Bitter Harvest: U.S. Foreign Policy and Afghanistan* (2003), the *Historical Dictionary of U.S. Diplomacy Since the Cold War* (2007) and *9/11 and the Wars in Afghanistan and Iraq: A Chronology and Reference Guide* (2011). His more recent edited collections include: *America's War on Terror* (2003; second edition 2009), *Judging Bush* (2009), and *The Obama Presidency: A Preliminary Assessment* (2012). Dr. Lansford has served as the editor of the annual *Political Handbook of the World* since 2012.

PHOTO CREDITS